An ALICE IN BIBLELAND® Storybook

# The LORD'S PRAYER

Written by Alice Joyce Davidson
Designed by Victoria Marshall

Text copyright © 1989 by Alice Joyce Davidson
Art copyright © 1989 by The C.R. Gibson Company
Published by The C.R. Gibson Company
Norwalk, Connecticut 06856
Printed in the United States of America

The C.R. Gibson Company, Norwalk, Connecticut 06856

A little girl named Alice
Went traveling in the West.

The rolling hills and mountains
Were the parts that she liked best.

One day she sat down on a stump
Among some giant trees,

And read a Bible story
From a book held on her knees.

She chose to read of Jesus
And the things He had to say

When He climbed up on a mountain
With His followers one day.

He talked to them of blessings,
He spoke to them of love,

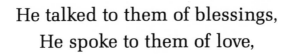

And taught them to pray simply
To our Father up above.

Alice sat there, thinking,
"I'd really like to share

This simple prayer that Jesus taught
With people everywhere."

The prayer is called "The Lord's Prayer."
Alice copied down each thought,

Then wrote a simple prayer herself
To help explain each thought.

*Our Father...*

God, You're like a parent.
You teach us and You guide us,
And like a loving parent,
You're always there beside us...

You listen to our problems,
You forgive the wrongs we do,

And life is so much happier
When we are close to You.

Who art in heaven . . .

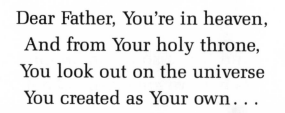

Dear Father, You're in heaven,
And from Your holy throne,
You look out on the universe
You created as Your own . . .

And though Your throne's in heaven,
We know we're in Your care,

We feel Your Holy Spirit
All around us everywhere.

Hallowed be Thy name. . .

We call You Lord, we call You God,
We call You Father, too,
And all of these are holy names.
They all belong to You..

And when we use Your name in prayer,
We feel a special glow,

A happy holy feeling
Because You love us so!

*Thy Kingdom come...*

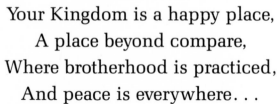

Your Kingdom is a happy place,
A place beyond compare,
Where brotherhood is practiced,
And peace is everywhere...

And if we open up our hearts
And follow Jesus' way,

We help to bring Your Kingdom
Here on earth to stay!

*Thy will be done on earth*
*as it is in heaven . . .*

Dear Father, You're the ruler
Both of heaven and of earth.
Your Holy Spirit guides us
From the moment of our birth . . .

You gave to us the Scriptures
So we may know Your ways.

Help us to know Your holy will
And bless us all our days.

*Give us this day our daily bread...*

We thank You, Father, for each day,
And for the food You give,
For a family that's loving,
And a happy place to live...

Not only do You keep us warm,
And happy, and well fed,

You give us things to do and learn—
All this is daily bread.

*And forgive us our debts...*

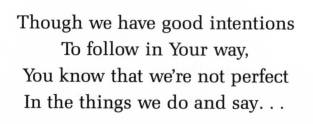

Though we have good intentions
To follow in Your way,
You know that we're not perfect
In the things we do and say...

And when we slip, dear Father,
You forgive the things we do,

You help us wash away our sins,
So we can start anew.

*As we forgive our debtors...*

Sometimes other people
Bring sadness to our days.
They lie to us or hurt us,
Or act in thoughtless ways...

When they ask us to forgive them,
There's just one thing to do—

We must follow Your example,
And be forgiving, too.

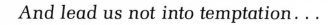

*And lead us not into temptation...*

We try to follow in Your way,
But as we go along,
We find that we can choose between
The right way and the wrong...

And though we find temptations,
Wherever we may go,

We know You're near us, Father,
To remind us to say, "No!"

*But deliver us from evil...*

Whenever we have problems,
Or troubles come our way,
We know that You are listening,
And hear us as we pray...

All through each day You guide us
Away from things that harm,

And when we go to sleep at night,
We feel safe in Your arms.

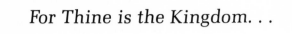

*For Thine is the Kingdom. . .*

Your Kingdom is the universe.
You rule the land and sea.
You're the King of every star,
And every galaxy. . .

You rule the earth on which we live,
You rule each living thing—

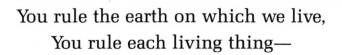

Your Kingdom is the universe,
And You are a loving King!

And the power, and the glory, for ever.

Dear God, before our world began,
You used Your mighty power
To make each detail of the earth,
Down to the smallest flower. . .

Now every minute, every day
You make the whole world new—

Your Kingdom is forever—
Glory, glory, God, to You.

Our Father
who art in heaven,
Hallowed be Thy name.
Thy Kingdom come.
Thy will be done on earth,
as it is in heaven.
Give us this day our daily bread,
and forgive us our debts,
as we forgive our debtors.
And lead us not into temptation,
but deliver us from evil:
For Thine is the Kingdom,
and the power,
and the glory,
for ever.
Amen